SWU-NAP- 005

SPANISH SOLDIERS DURING THE NAPOLEONIC WARS 1797-1808

SOLDIERSHOP PUBLISHING

Spanish soldiers during the Napoleonic wars 1797-1808 redact by Luca Stefano Cristini
First edition December 2019
ISBN code: 978-88-93275286

Luca Cristini Editore per i tipi Soldiershop, via Orio 35/4 - 24050 Zanica (BG) ITALY. wwwsoldiershop.com

SPANISH SOLDIERS DURING THE NAPOLEONIC WARS 1797-1808

CONTENTS

▲ The family of Carlos IV king of Spain, portrait by Francisco Goya

THE SPANISH ARMY FROM 1792 TO 1808

In the late 18th century, Bourbon-ruled Spain had an alliance with Bourbon-ruled France and therefore did not have to fear a land war. Its only serious enemy was Britain, which had a powerful Royal Navy; Spain, therefore, concentrated its resources on its Navy. When the French Revolution overthrew the Bourbons, a land war with France became a danger which the king tried to avoid. The Spanish Army was ill-prepared. The officer corps was selected primarily on the basis of royal patronage, rather than merit. About a third of the junior officers had been promoted from the ranks, and they did have talent, but they had few opportunities for promotion or leadership. The rank-and-file were poorly trained peasants. Elite units included foreign regiments of Irishmen, Italians, Swiss, and Walloons, in addition to elite artillery and engineering units. Equipment was old-fashioned and in disrepair. The army lacked its own horses, oxen, and mules for transportation, so these auxiliaries were operated by civilians, who might run away if conditions looked bad. In combat,

▲ Carlos IV king of Spain, portrait by Francisco Bayeu

small units fought well, but their old-fashioned tactics were hard of use against the French *Grande Armée*, despite repeated desperate efforts at last-minute reform. When war broke out with France in 1808, the army was deeply unpopular. Leading generals were assassinated, and the army proved too incompetent to handle command and control. Junior officers from peasant families deserted and went over to the insurgents; many units disintegrated. Spain was unable to mobilize its artillery or cavalry. The Spain of the end of the XVIII century was dominated by the complex personality of Manuel Godoy.

Manuel Godoy

Manuel Godoy y Álvarez de Faria, Prince of Peace, 1st Duke of Alcudia, 1st Duke of Sueca, 1st Baron of Mascalbó (1767 –1851) was First Secretary of State of Spain from 1792 to 1797 and from 1801 to 1808. He received many titles, including *Príncipe de la Paz* ("Prince of Peace"), by which he is widely known. He came to power at a young age as the favorite of the King and Queen. Despite multiple disasters, he maintained power. Many Spanish leaders blamed Godoy for the disastrous war with Britain that cut off Spain's Empire and ruined its finances. Godoy has been one of the only two people in history (the other being Baldomero Espartero) to have held the title of "Prince" in the Kingdom of Spain, a dignity traditionally reserved for the heir to the throne.

GODOY REFORMS

After the war against the French Republic in 1793-95 and the peace treaty signed between Spain and France, the Godoy government pursued a firm policy of disarmament. All the military aspects of the army were so neglected that when it was necessary to organize the invasion operations of Portugal in 1801 an army of operations for the invasion of Portugal in 1801, they were a complete failure. After the disastrous campaign, Godoy then began a profound modernization of the army, which finally gave good results in the military campaigns of the Spanish Division under the command of the Marquis de la Romana sent to Denmark and in the subsequent battles of the War of Independence. Advised by a distinguished group of officers, including Lieutenant General Don José Urrutia, Morla, Pardo de Figueroa and the Marquis de Casa-Cagigal, Godoy actively devoted himself to developing a reform plan, based on the following organizational rules of the military forces :

- Royal decree of Quinta, dated 27 October 1800.

- Artillery reform, of 22 July 1802, with which the Royal Artillery Corps was reorganized into five

▲ Agustin Esteve y Marqués Manuel Godoy

regiments, three fixed companies, five workers' companies and four invalids, for a total of 7,522 men.

- General infantry regulation of 26 August 1802, which reorganizes the infantry weapon in 33 Spanish line regiments and 12 light battalions, for a total of 100,000 men.

- Regulation of the cavalry, of 30 January 1803 and subsequent decree of its reorganization of 1805, for which it establishes for the cavalry weapon a force of 12 regiments of line, 6 regiments of hussars and 6 regiments of hunters, for a total of 16,200 men and 13,000 horses.

- Engineers Ordinance of 11 July 1803, which reorganizes the Royal Corps of Engineers with a staff of 196 officers; creates the Royal Regiment of Mining Sappers with a staff of 1,275 men; and creates the Academy of Engineers in Alcalá de Henares.

- Creation of a Royal Academy of Officers in Zamora, in 1805.

Adding the troops of the Royal House, the foreign regiments and the provincial militia, the Spanish army, restructured by Godoy, reached a strength of about 180,000 men, superior to both the old Spanish forces and those of the French army, formed by about 110,000 men beginning of the 1793 war.

THE SPANISH ARMY OF 1808

The Spanish army of 1,808 consisted of 198 infantry battalions and 126 squadrons of cavalry, directed by 8.0000 officers and 131.000 troops, totaling about 139.000 men distributed as follows:

87,201 soldiers and infantry officers.
16,623 soldiers and cavalry officers.
10,960 horses.
6,971 soldiers and artillery officers.
1,223 soldiers and engineering officers.
32,418 soldiers and officers of provincial militias.
The units were articulated as follows:

Royal House Troops
Spanish line infantry
Foreign Line Infantry
Light infantry
Provincial militias
Chivalry
Royal Artillery Corps
Royal Corps of Engineers

After the national uprising against the French in May 1,808, these forces were articulated in seven armies of operations under the orders of the different Provisional Boards that were emerging throughout the national territory:

Andalusian Army
Aragon Army
Catalonian Army
Army of Old Castile
Extremadura Army
Galicia Army
Valencia Army

CAVALRY REGIMENT IN 1797				
Regiment	Coat	Collar	Cuffs	Lapels
Rey	white	Violet	Violet	Violet
Reyna	white	Violet	White	Violet
Principe	white	Violet	Violet	White
Infante	white	White	Violet	White
Borbon	white	Scarlet	Scarlet	White
Farnesio	white	Scarlet	White	White
Alcantara	white	Green	Green	Green
Espana	white	Black	Black	Black
Algarve	white	Buff	Scarlet	Scarlet
Calatrava	white	Scarlet	Scarlet	Scarlet
Santiago	white	Crimson	Crimson	Crimson
Montesa	white	Bleu	Bleu	Bleu
Maria Luisa	white	Light bleu	Lighr bleu	Light bleu

INFANTRY REGIMENT IN 1797

Regiment	Coat	Collar	Cuffs	Lapels	Buttons
Rey	white	Scarlet	Violet	Violet	Brass
Reyna	white	Scarlet	Scarlet	White	Brass
Principe	white	Violet	Violet	Violet	Silver
Saboya	white	Black	Black	Black	Silver
Corona	white	Bleu	Bleu	Bleu	Silver
Africa	white	White	Black	Black	Brass
Zamora	white	Black	Black	White	Brass
Soria	white	Violet	Violet	White	Silver
Cordoba	white	Violet	Scarlet	Scarlet	Brass
Guadalajara	white	Scarlet	Scarlet	Scarlet	Silver
Sevilla	white	Black	Scarlet	Black	Brass
Granada	white	Green	Buff	Buff	Brass
Valencia	white	Buff	Scarlet	Scarlet	Silver
Zaragossa	white	Green	Green	White	Brass
Espana	white	Green	Green	Green	Brass
Toledo	white	Scarlet	Lighr blue	Light bleu	Brass
Mallorca	white	Buff	Scarlet	Scarlet	Brass
Burgos	white	White	Violet	Violet	Silver
Murcia	white	Light bleu	Light bleu	White	Brass
Leon	white	White	Scarlet	Scarlet	Silver
Cantabria	white	Light bleu	Light bleu	Light bleu	Silver
Asturias	white	White	Light bleu	Light bleu	Brass
Fijo de Ceuta	white	Green	Green	White	Silver
Navarra	white	Scarlet	Light bleu	Light bleu	Silver
Aragon	white	Green	Scarlet	Scarlet	Brass
America	white	Violet	Buff	Buff	Silver
Princesa	white	White	Scarlet	White	Brass
Extrenadura	white	Scarlet	Buff	Buff	Silver
Malaga	white	Buff	Buff	Buff	Silver
Jaen	white	Scarlet	Black	Black	Silver
Ordonnes Militares	white	Scarlet	Scarlet	White	Silver
Voluntarios de Castilla	white	Crimson	Crimson	Crimson	Silver
Voluntarios del Estado	Bleu	bleu	Buff	Buff	Silver
Borbon	Bleu	Scarlet	Scarlet	Light bleu	Brass

INFANTRY FOREIGN REGIMENT IN 1797

Regiment	Coat	Collar	Cuffs	Lapels	Buttons
Irlanda (Irish)	white	Scarlet	Scarlet	Scarlet	Silver
Hibernia (Irish)	white	Green	Scarlet	Scarlet	Silver
Ultonia (Irish)	white	Scarlet	Green	White	Brass
Kruter (Swiss)	Bleu	Yellow	Scarlet	Scarlet	Silver
San Gall (Swiss)	Bleu	Scarlet	Scarlet	Scarlet	Silver
Reding (Swiss)	Bleu	Yellow	Scarlet	Scarlet	Silver
Betschart (Swiss)	Bleu	Scarlet	Yellow	Yellow	Silver
Neaples (Italy)	white	Light bleu	Scarlet	Scarlet	Silver
Yann (Swiss)	Bleu	Scarlet	Scarlet	Scarlet	Brass
Courten (Swiss)	Bleu	Bleu	Scarlet	Scarlet	Silver

THE COLOUR PLATES

THE CAVALRY 1750–1797

Compañía Española Americana

Compañía Flamenca

Compañía Italiana

Compañía de Moros Mogataces de Zeuta; fue formada en Oran el año de 1734, y tambien ay sierto n.º de a pie.

Spanish. cavalry foreign company 1750-1790

Reyna 1755.
Por privilegio tiene este lugar.

Lusitania 1709.

Almanza 1701.

Sagunto 1703.

Spanish. cavalry regiment 1750-1790

Villaviciosa, 1689.

Pavia, 1684.

Almansa, 1676.

Regimientos de Dragones de tres Esquadrones cada Esquadron Consta de tres Compañias, y estas

Spanish. cavalry regiment 1750-1790

Usares Españoles. 1795.

Spanish hussar 1795-97

Regimientos de Cavalleria de tres Esquadrones Cada Esquadron consta de tres Compañias, y estas de 60 Cavallos cada vna; Rey. fue creado Año. 1538.

Cavalry regiment Rey 1797

Reyna, 1703.
Por privilegio sigue al del Rey.

Cavalry regiment Reyna 1797

Principe, 1703.
Por priviltoio tiete, este lugar.

Cavalry regiment Principe 1797

16

Infante, 1642.
Por privilegio tiene este lugar.

Cavalry regiment Infante 1797

26

Regimientos de quatro Esquadrones Costa de Granada fue creado año. 1735.

Cavalry regiment Borbon 1797

Voluntarios, 1762.

Cavalry regiment Farnesio 1797

27

Alcantara, 1656.

Cavalry regiment Alcantara 1797

España, 1659.

Cavalry regiment Espana 1797

Algarve, 1797.

Cavalry regiment Algarve 1797

Calatrava, 1703.

Cavalry regiment Calatrava 1797

Santiago, 1703.

Cavalry regiment Santiago 1797

Montesa, 1706.

Cavalry regiment Montesa 1797

Reyna Maria Luisa fue creado Año de 1793.

Cavalry regiment Reyna maria Luisa 1797

THE COLOUR PLATES

THE INFANTRY AND THE FOREIGN REGIMENTS 1750–1797

7

Regimientos de Ynfanteria, de tres Batallones
cada Batall.n consta de sinco Compañias, inclusa
vna de Granaderos, y estas de 160 Plazas, y todos
llevan en el boton del vniforme, el nombre del suyo
Rey. su creacion Ynmemorial.

Infantry regiment Rey 1797

Reyna, 1537.

Infantry regiment Reyna 1797

Principe, 1537.

Infantry regiment Principe 1797

Saboya, 1537.

Infantry regiment Saboya 1797

Corona, 1537.

Infantry regiment Corona 1797

Africa, 1537.

Infantry regiment Africa 1797

Zamora, 1580.

Infantry regiment Zamora 1797

13

Soria, 1597.

Infantry regiment Soria 1797

Cordova, 1650.

Infantry regiment Cordoba 1797

Guadalaxara, 1657.

Infantry regiment Guadalajara 1797

Sevilla. 1657.

Infantry regiment Sevilla 1797

Granada, 1657.

Infantry regiment Granada 1797

Valencia, 1658.

Infantry regiment Valencia 1797

Zaraooza, 1660.

Infantry regiment Zaragossa 1797

Espana, 1660.

Infantry regiment Espana 1797

Toledo, 1661.

Infantry regiment Toledo 1797

Mallorca, 1682.

Infantry regiment Mallorca 1797

Burgos, 1694.

Infantry regiment Burgos 1797

Murcia, 1694.

Infantry regiment Murcia 1797

Leon, 1694.

Infantry regiment Leon 1797

Cantabria, 1703.

Infantry regiment Cantabria 1797

Asturias, 1703.

Infantry regiment Asturias 1797

Fixò de Zeuta, 1703.

Infantry regiment Fijo de Ceuta 1797

Navarra, 1705.

Infantry regiment Navarra 1797

Aragon, 1797.

Infantry regiment Aragon 1797

America, 1764.

Infantry regiment America 1797

Princesa, 1766.

Infantry regiment Princesa 1797

Extremadura. 1766.

Infantry regiment Extremadura 1797

37

Malaga. 1797.

Infantry regiment Malaga 1797

Jaen, 1793.

Infantry regiment Jaen 1797

Ordenes Militares. 1793.

Infantry regiment Ordenes Militares 1797

Voluntarios de Castilla, 1793.

Infantry regiment Voluntarios de Castilla 1797

Granaderos Voluntarios de Estado fueron creados Año de 1794.

Infantry regiment Voluntarios de Estado 1797

Borbon, 1796.

Infantry regiment Borbon 1797

Irlanda, 1698.

Foreign Infantry regiment Irlanda (Irish) 1797

Hibernia, 1709.

Foregin Infantry regiment Hibernia (Irish) 1797

Ultonia, 1709.

Foreign Infantry regiment Ultonia (Irish) 1797

Ynfanteria Suiza
Schwaller, fue creado Año, de 1734.

Foreign Infantry regiment Schwaller (Swiss) 1797

San Gall Rutiman Año, de 1742.

Foreign Infantry regiment San Gall (Swiss) 1797

Reding año, de 1742.

Foreign Infantry Reding (Swiss) 1797

Vacante de Betschart Año 1742.

Foreign Infantry regiment Betschart (Swiss) 1797

Infanteria Ytaliana; Napoles. fue creado año. 1572.

Foreign Infantry regiment Naples (Italy) 1797

Yann. año, de 1794

Foreign Infantry regiment Yann (Swiss) 1797

Courten. Año, de 1796.

Foreign Infantry regiment (Swiss) 1797

Real Guardia de Alabarderos, Consta esta Compañia de 550. Plazas fue creada año de 1707. y se compone de Sargentos qᵉ an Servido con onrades en el Exto.

Real Guardia de Alabarders de palacio 1797

THE COLOUR PLATES

THE LIGHT INFANTRY MILITIA AND OTHER 1750–1797

Cazadores de Infanteria de Guardias Españolas.
fueron creados Año, 1793. y en cada Batallon ay vna
Compañia sobre el mismo pie que el de las demas.

Guard Infantry foot chasseur 1797

Cazadores Voluntarios de la Corona Año, de 1795.

Volunteer of la Corona 1797

Guardias de Ynfanteria Española; Consta este Reoim-
ento de seis Batallones, cada vno de ocho Compañias, in-
clusa vna de Cazadores, y la fuerza de cada vna de cien
Plazas fue creado el Año, de 1704.

Guard regiment grenadier 1797

Ynfanteria Lijera
Primero de Cataluña, fue creado Año de 1762 consta
de vn Batallon.

Light infantry Battalion Primero de Cataluna 1797

Primero de Voluntarios de Aragon, fue creado Año de 1762. y consta de vn Batallon.

Light infantry Battalion Primero de Aragon 1797

Segundo de Voluntarios de Aragon fue creado año de 1793. y consta de vn Batallon.

Light infantry Battalion Segundo de Aragon 1797

Scaundo de Voluntarios de Cataluña, fue creado año 476.
Voluntarios de Tarragona, Idem de Gerona creados año .
Segundo de Voluntarios de Barcelona creado Año, de 575
Todos constan de vn Batallon.

Light infantry Battalion segundo de Cataluna 1797

Voluntarios de Balbastro, fue creado Año. 5794. y Consta de vn Batallon.

Light infantry Battalion Voluntarios de Balbastro 1797

Voluntarios de Valencia Creados Año, de 1794.

Light infantry Battalion Coluntarios de Valencia 1797

Compañia fixa en el campo de Gibraltar la de Escopeteros de Getares de Infantería, formada el Año, de 1705.

Light infantry Company el campo de Gibraltar 1797

19

Compañia suelta de Fusileros en Aragon.

Light infantry Company fusilier de Aragon 1797

En Zeuta cinco Compañias formadas el año, de 1762.

Light infantry Battalion de Zeuta (Ceuta) 1797

Ynfanteria de Marina, Consta este Cuerpo de 12384 Pla-
zas, inclusos los Jovenes, distribuidas en doce Batallones
de a seis Compañias, con quatro oficiales cada vna, y vn coman-
dante con dos Ayudantes por Batallon.

1797

Navy infantry 1797

*Melicias Provinciales, Constan estos Cuerpos de 42 Regi-
mientos, Compuestos todos de vn solo Batallon sobre el
pie. de los Veteranos, y fueron creados en dos ocasiones à saver
28 en el año 1734. Y los 34 restantes en el Año de 1766.*

Militia provinciales 1797

41

Cuerpo de Ingenieros Creados Año, de 1711.

Royal engineers officer 1797

42

Real Cuerpo de Artilleria; se creo este en Regimiento
el Año, de 1770. y consta, de seis Batallones, cada
vno de siete Compañias, y estas de 108. Plazas.

Artillery Regiment 1797

Artilleria Volante, ò acaballo de Reales Guardias de
Corps, Consta esta Compañia de 54 hombres, fue creada
Año, de 1797.

Company of Horse Artillery of the Guard 1797

THE COLOUR PLATES

VARIOUS
1806–1808

Officier of Regiment of infantru Rey and officer of Almansa hussar regiment

Soldiers of Zamora regiment. At righr catalan officer

fusilier and grenadier of infantry regiment

Engineers soldiers and artillery officer

Asturia Dragoons officer and private, at right heavy cavalrymen

Hussar, dragoons and hevay cavalry soldiers

Grenadier and guard infantry regiment

SOLDIERS, WEAPONS & UNIFORMS ALREADY PUBLISHED
(SOME TITLES)